THE IMMORTAL
ELVIS PRESLEY
1935-1977

THE IMMORTAL
ELVIS PRESLEY
1935-1977

JOSEPH ADAIR

LONGMEADOW
PRESS

Published by Longmeadow Press,
201 High Ridge Road, Stamford, CT 06904.
All rights reserved. No part of this book may be
reproduced or utilized in any form or by
any means, electronic or mechanical, including
photocopying, recording or by any information
storage and retrieval system, without permission
in writing from the Publisher.

Copyright © 1992 Reed International Books Limited

ISBN 0-681-41519-3

Printed in Singapore

09876543

Contents

Memphis and Music

YOU'D HAVE TO LOOK HARD to find a more impoverished corner of depression-hit America than East Tupelo, Mississippi, in 1935. Yet the birth of Elvis Aron, only surviving son of Gladys and Vernon, Presley on 8 January was an event that would ultimately enrich American and world culture. For in the story of popular music, Elvis Presley's name was to be written first and largest.

He tied together the threads of white country and black blues to create rock 'n' roll: the reverberations of the fusion still echo today. He polarized everyone on both sides of the generation gap, wrenching pop music from the hands of the older generation and giving it to America's youth. For many, he was and is The King.

Elvis's early childhood was no different from that of other young Americans growing up in the shadow of a world war being waged far from home shores. As he reached his early teens, music was to replace cowboy outfits as the love of his life – and like so many great singers, the youngster's introduction to music was through religion. 'The Church gave me the only singing training I ever had,' he later cheerfully admitted. 'All the rest came naturally.' It is, perhaps, the ultimate irony that as Elvis' career developed the Church would be in the forefront of the anti-rock 'n' roll movement.

Elvis was as close to his parents as any only child. He was in fact a twin, but the younger of the two, Jesse Garon, was born dead. 'Many folk believe that when one twin dies the other grows up with all the qualities of the other,' Elvis remarked later. 'If that did happen to me, then I'm lucky.'

In the early Forties he gave his first public performance while still at school, singing 'Old Shep' and winning the five-dollar second prize at the Mississippi-Alabama Fair and Dairy Show as well as a subsequent broadcast on the local radio station, WELO. In contrast to his later microphone-toting, hip-swivelling antics, this was a relatively sedate rendition, performed both unaccompanied and un-amplified, and while standing on a chair! Little did anyone know they were listening to one of the biggest music stars of the future.

The segregated South gave few opportunities for white and black musicians to mix, so each kept to their own. Yet the innumerable radio stations sprouting up across the region were accessible to all – and, whether by accident or design, the young Presley started tuning in to a variety of musical sounds and styles.

The artists he preferred and those whose records he borrowed from neighbours and friends (being too poor to buy his own) were instructive; they lay both sides of the colour line and encompassed country artists (the traditionally based Jimmie Rodgers and Roy Acuff) and bluesmen (BB King, Rufus Thomas and Howlin' Wolf, who often cut their songs live on air). It was these black and white musical roots Elvis was to link for all time, together with a touch of James Dean, to create dynamite.

When Elvis was 13, the family moved to Memphis, where they took rooms above a rabbi in a house at 462 Alabama Street. 'We were flat broke in Tupelo,' he recalled, 'so my dad packed our belongings into boxes and put them into our 1939 Plymouth…we decided that things had to get better.' His father

couldn't seem to hold down a job in Tupelo and figured that Memphis offered more opportunities.

Money was tight...but the gift of a twelve-dollar guitar from his father *(above right,* with dog), the money raised by a voluntary smoking ban, gave Elvis his chance to copy the music he heard on the radio and those borrowed records. At first, few of his new school friends at LC Humes High School would have guessed Elvis would be a national star before he even turned 21. A quiet, reserved boy, he retreated even further into his shell when he took on a night-shift job at a local factory to help out financially at home; in fact, he found it hard to stay awake in class. But when a microphone was put in his hand, young Presley didn't just wake up – he came alive. His emotionally-charged rendition of 'Cold Cold Icy Fingers' at the school's 1952 Christmas concert stopped the show, while the encore of 'Till I Waltz Again With You' won rapturous applause, much to his surprise.

From then on, Elvis never looked back, as fellow Humes High pupil Johnny Burnette, himself a future rock 'n' roll star, recalled. 'Every now and then Elvis would go to one of the cafés or bars and slouch across a chair. He never sat up straight, he just sort of lay there with that mean look on his face. Then some folk would say "Let's hear you sing, boy", and ol' El would stroll up to the most convenient spot, looking at the ground all the time. Then all of a sudden he'd slide that guitar round to his front and near raise the roof...'

Leaving school in 1953 with a professional singing career still only a pipedream, Elvis joined a toolmaking company before settling down to a $1.25-an-hour truck-driving job for Crown Electric. With his luxuriant sideburns and unruly mop of jet-black hair, he could be seen driving around and dropping off various loads. It's unlikely he had cause to visit the Sun Record Company's recording studios: signposted as the Memphis Recording Service, it was run by local entrepreneur Sam Phillips, who was prepared to record anything – from weddings to business functions – for money. He even offered a walk-in 'record yourself' service: for just four dollars, you could walk out with your very own one-off record.

It was Elvis's devotion to his mother (*below*) that took him from school hops and veterans shows to the recording studio: he paid his first visit to Sam Phillips' premises with the intention of cutting a

demo disc for Gladys Presley's birthday. It was April 1953 and Presley just 18 when he walked in, laid the proceeds of three and a half hours behind the wheel on the counter and shyly announced his intention to cover the Inkspots' 'My Happiness' and 'That's Where Your Heartaches Begin', accompanying himself on guitar. Phillips' assistant, Marian Keisker, was on duty, and intuition later led her to play the tape she made to her boss. What he heard knocked him out – and put Elvis Presley on the first rung of the ladder to fame and fortune.

Sunrise to Stardom

SAM PHILLIPS HAD always dreamed of a 'white boy who could sing black' – and Elvis was the answer to the small-time label owner's prayer. Yet initially he found problems deciding which setting his rough diamond would sound best in. Elvis's first attempt at recording, a song called 'Without You' – written, so legend has it, by an inmate of the Tennessee State Penitentiary – proved disastrous, while Phillips' request for Elvis to show him what he could sing led to a total mish-mash of styles from R&B to Dean Martin and back again. Gospel was Elvis's real love at the time, and he'd often visit the Memphis Auditorium to stand up and sing unaccompanied. This was, however, hardly stuff of which fortunes were made.

Phillips found a winning combination in teaming Presley with guitarist Scotty Moore and Moore's neighbour, upright bass-slapper Bill Black (*left*). One Saturday afternoon in June 1954 the trio, billed as the Blue Moon Boys (*below*), met at Scotty's house, obeying Phillips' curt instruction to 'go develop a style'.

The result was history. Raw, spare and spine-tingling, the elements of Presley's voice and frantically scrubbing acoustic guitar plus Moore's quicksilver electric guitar and Black's percussive bass added up to primal excitement of a level never previously experienced. Even so, Elvis wasn't entirely convinced he had a future at Sun, and to cover his tracks he auditioned for the gospel group the Songfellows. Luckily for pop music, they didn't want him and Elvis signed to the Sun label on 19 July 1954 for three years.

The trio's first recording session took place over three days in Sun's studio, and got progressively wilder...not to mention hotter! Five titles were committed to magnetic tape before the musicians took a break. Refreshed, they crashed into a breakneck version of 'That's All Right', a raw blues originally recorded by Arthur Crudup. A startled Sam Phillips immediately insisted they do it again...this time with the tape rolling!

The acetate test record that resulted was first aired on local station WHBQ by disc jockey Dewey Phillips (no relation to Sam). WHBQ's (mostly white) listeners assumed Elvis was black, as the majority of artists on Phillips' show were: the truth was established when a torrent of listener reaction forced a nervous Presley out of the cinema where he'd been hiding and into the studio for a revealing interview. By the time the week was out, orders of a staggering 5,000 copies had been registered for a record Sam Phillips hadn't even pressed! Nine days later, the song (backed by another cut from the same session, 'Blue Moon of Kentucky') was well on its way to selling 20,000 copies: Elvis Presley had arrived!

Gospel remained an abiding musical influence – and one Elvis shared with many other artists on the Sun Records roster. With studio time in Sam Phillips' primitive shack in more than ample supply, it wasn't unusual for artists like Elvis, Johnny Cash, Jerry Lee Lewis and Carl Perkins to get together for an after-hours singalong of sacred songs from their child-hood. Years later, the best of these tapes were compiled and issued under the appropriate title of the *Million Dollar Quartet.* The priceless foursome are pictured above: from left, Lewis, Perkins, Presley (at piano) and Cash.

When the trio of Presley, Moore and Black went out live, the money was split 50 per cent to the singer and 25 per cent each to the other two, and with 'That's All Right' reaching Number Three in the local country-music chart, gigs were scarcely hard to come by…million dollar or otherwise!

Elvis quit his truck-driving job and, his hopes buoyed by a *Billboard* review rating him 'a potent new chanter who can clearly sock over a tune', was soon socking it to his public with a second single, Roy Brown's 'Good Rockin' Tonight'. This, together with the subsequent 'Milkcow Blues Boogie' from the pen of Sleepy John Estes, cemented his reputation as 1955 dawned, and appearances on *Louisiana Hayride* and *Grand Ole Opry,* country music's two most famous radio shows, broadcast his name far beyond the Memphis area.

Arkansas, Louisiana and Texas all played host to the South's hottest star. Scotty Moore, who had hitherto combined strumming with the manager's job, willingly gave way on the latter count to Memphis DJ Bob Neal. A pink Ford and a pink Cadillac joined the famous pink jacket as Elvis defined the rock star lifestyle that so many others were to crave…and that was ultimately to prove his undoing.

Presley's first national hit came with 'Baby Let's Play House', a rockabilly-flavoured uptempo number that made the country Top Ten. Only one further release, 'Mystery Train', was to follow on Sun before Elvis moved on to bigger things. The new driving force behind the young ex-trucker was a certain Colonel Tom Parker.

If Elvis's early life had been influenced by his parents, then Parker was the man who took over as the major influence in his adult years. Some decades later it was suggested that Parker's own early life story had been somewhat different than previously believed and that he was a Dutch immigrant christened Cornelis van Kuijk. Despite military service in the Thirties, his title of Colonel had, it was said, been conferred rather more recently by the ex-country singer governor of Kentucky. Notwithstanding this, he ran his young protégé's career like a military operation, having graduated from running carnival shows to managing country acts like Hank Snow and Eddy Arnold.

It was Parker (*below*) who realized that television would put Presley on the map nationwide. And it was Parker, too, who negotiated the move from local Sun Records to the giant RCA Records in New York, the ideal vehicle to spread the Presley gospel worldwide. The then-massive fee of $40,000 was $15,000 higher than the rival Atlantic bid, and was seen as quite a risk for the label; subsequent events proved it one of the great bargains of music history.

On 10 January 1956 Elvis recorded 'Heartbreak Hotel' with Moore and Black, now augmented by drummer D.J. Fontana and the Jordanaires, a vocal backing group. On 28 January Elvis made the first of six TV appearances to push the single, and at the end of February it appeared in *Billboard's* Hot Hundred. By April, when 'Heartbreak Hotel' topped the chart, Presley accounted for 50 per cent of RCA's pop record sales. His first LP became RCA's biggest ever album on advance orders alone.

Television appearances mounted: Tommy and Jimmy Dorsey's *Stage Show*, the *Steve Allen Show,* Ed Sullivan's *Toast of the Town* (on which Elvis's 'suggestive' hip movements were cut out of camera shot), Milton Berle…Elvis became the guest to have. Elvis was diffident about his style. When asked if he intended arousing the females in his audience, he answered, 'That's just the way I sing. I can't sing any other way. I need my whole body.'

Elvis and Uncle Sam

IF TELEVISION EXPOSURE had been the making of Elvis Presley, then the Hollywood movie machine was to take his reputation and magnify it on an unparalleled worldwide scale.

Elvis was signed by Hal Wallis of Paramount Pictures for $450,000 to star in three motion pictures. His first year in films saw him fulfil his three-picture contract – and all were box-office smashes. *Love Me Tender* (1956), *Loving You* (1957) and *Jailhouse Rock* (1957) (his first film in colour, *left*) each recouped their million-dollar-plus costs in a matter of weeks; *Love Me Tender* (previously *The Reno Brothers*) was even renamed after his title song. *Loving You* provided the opportunity to perform seven songs as truck-driver-turned-rock star Deke Rivers.

But it was *Jailhouse Rock* (*poster right*) that climaxed the year, its unforgettable title song and the visuals that went with it creating rock film's first classic production number.

Jailhouse Rock

King Creole (*right*) was the first film of 1958, but very nearly didn't happen when the King was called up by the US Army. His induction was postponed for two all-important months to ensure that the $300,000 spent on pre-production was not wasted – and *King Creole,* which benefited from a Harold Robbins storyline, was unanimously acclaimed as Elvis's best film to date.

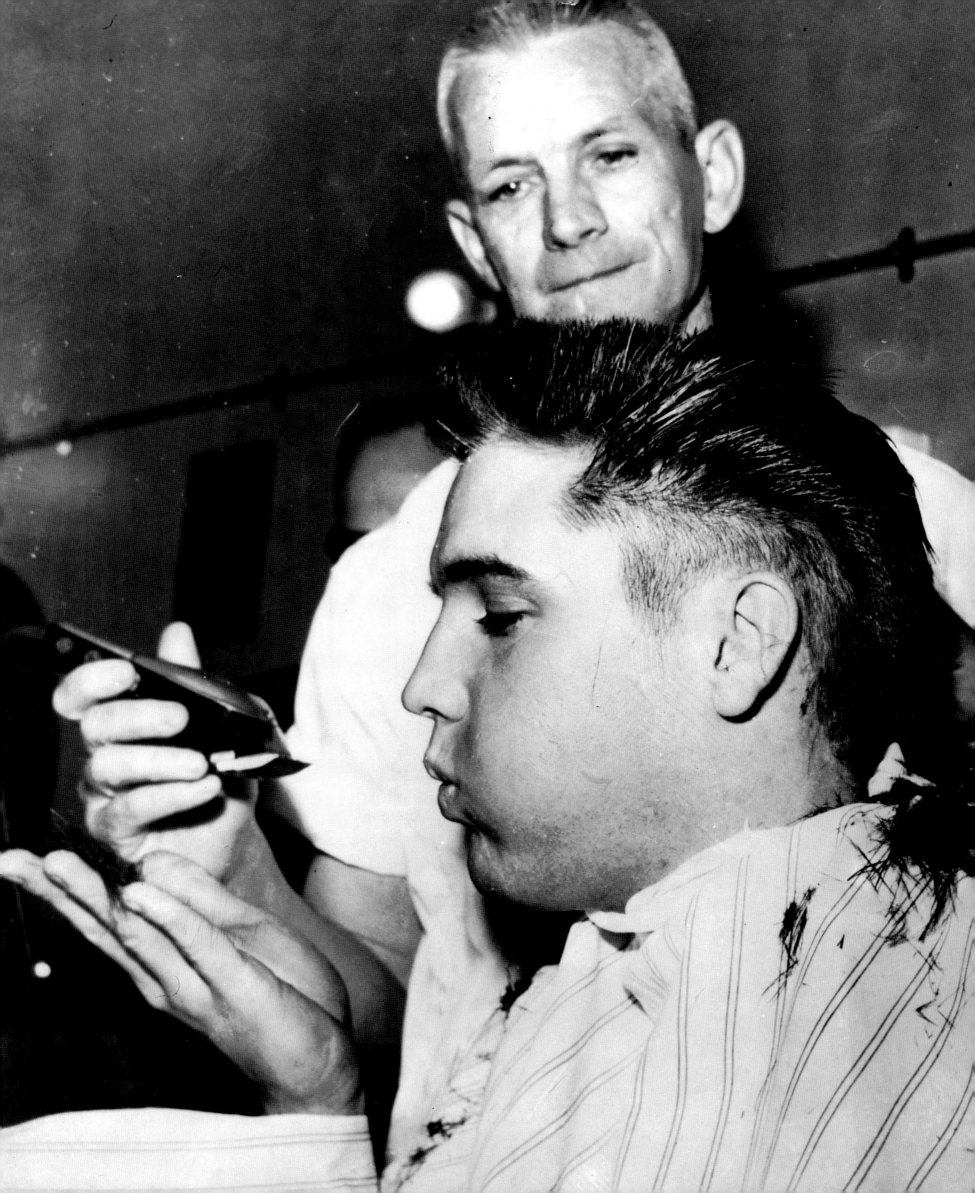

As soon as he knew that Elvis was bound for Europe, Parker had him spending his leave at RCA's Nashville studios, stockpiling tracks for later release. Hits issued during Elvis's tour of duty included 'Wear My Ring Around Your Neck', 'Hard-Headed Woman', the double-sided 'One Night'/'I Got Stung', 'A Fool Such As I' and 'Big Hunk of Love'.

A less conventional venture was 'Elvis Sails', a sound-track of Presley's departure on the troop-ship General Randall. Even less enduring were the novelty records, such as 'Bye Bye Elvis', that sought to cash in on the event.

Though Elvis's film career was masterminded by Paramount's Hal Wallis (*below*, at Elvis's screen test), *Love Me Tender*, co-starring Richard Egan and Debra Paget, had been cut at the Twentieth Century-Fox studios: subsequent films were also cut with MGM and United Artists.

At this stage it was by no means certain that Presley would·sweep the celluloid world before him: music critics, after all, had been vocal in their disapproval. Jack Gould of the *New York Times* concluded that 'Mr Presley has no discernible singing ability', while Jack O'Brien of the *New York Journal American* concluded that 'He can't sing a lick [and] makes up for vocal shortcomings with the weirdest, and plainly planned, suggested animation short of an aborigine's mating dance.'

Not that such high-powered criticism had one iota of effect on his popularity with the teen generation: 'Blue Suede Shoes' (written by former label-mate Carl Perkins) reached Number Twenty while 'Don't Be Cruel' went straight to the top, with the B-side 'Hound Dog' behind it at Number Two in its own right (the US charts are compiled by reference to airplay as well as sales).

Love Me Tender (*above*) gave Elvis the chance to sing four country-flavoured songs in a tale of the US Civil War. It was produced by David Weisbart, who'd had previous experience of teen idols when working with the late James Dean on *Rebel Without A Cause*. Indeed, Elvis had taken on Dean's mantle as the ultimate all-American hero – and though the film's plot was both slim and sentimental, the Presley presence saw the million-dollar production break even in just three weeks. The title song, too, was a chart success throughout the world and RCA cleverly initiated a string of sound-track records that provided a valuable spin-off: the movies plugged the records and vice versa. Meanwhile, back at Sun, Carl Perkins and Jerry Lee Lewis were stepping into Elvis's (blue suede) shoes, but the label was never to enjoy such success again.

Fans had flocked to the cinema in their thousands worldwide, but their idol was to be two years absent from the big screen. On the other hand, his induction into the US Army was the media event of 1958, as Colonel Parker and the US authorities worked hand in hand to derive benefit from the situation.

Elvis was inducted on 24 March 1958, bidding farewell to his parents (*above*) in favour of Uncle Sam. His pay was immediately reduced from $1000 per week to a mere $83.10 on his posting to Fort Chaffee, Arkansas.

It was the much-photographed cropping of those famous lank, black locks (*right*) that persuaded most fans that Private 53310761 Presley, E. would receive no special privileges; his hair was, however, burned to deter souvenir hunters. There were those who thought that two years out of the spotlight would see others take up where Elvis left off, and others who thought Elvis would never regain his crown. But they'd reckoned without Parker.

Elvis's broad shoulders were required to shoulder the good-natured jibes of his comrades and the attentions of German girl fans, who forced him to use the barracks as a retreat. Offered a chance to sing with Special Services, he indicated he'd rather remain an ordinary soldier.

If he resented the brakes being put on his meteoric rise, Elvis didn't show it. 'The officers expect discipline and respect and that's what I'll give them,' he insisted. The most distressing time for Elvis came when he was granted compassionate leave to be by his father's side after Gladys Presley's death from a heart attack on 14 August 1958.

Elvis's earnings in the previous year had enabled him to buy a $100,000 mansion, Graceland, where the family could make their home. Despite this, he'd temporarily moved his parents close to Fort Hood, Texas, where he was undergoing basic combat training with the 2nd Armoured Division. After Gladys's death, his father, Vernon, and grandmother, Minnie Mae, eventually moved to Germany to be within easy reach, while Elvis himself erected a ten-foot monument to his 'Mom' inscribed with the words:' She was the sunshine of our home.'

Presley's only musical appearance in fifteen months came at the Paris Lido when he was dragged on stage in June 1959 during an eight-day spell of leave. But elsewhere he was making a reputation as a good soldier, leading a three-man reconnaissance team in the US Army's 32nd Scout Platoon. Back home, many alternative teen heroes, including Fabian and Frankie Avalon, were promoted but no one artist made anything like a comparable impact.   Elvis himself didn't 'consider them rivals...there's room for everyone. And if other people can make it, good luck to them.'

Eight US Top Ten hits had helped keep him in the pop spotlight. Furthermore, many who had chosen to ignore Presley were now looking at him in a new light – the first step to his post-Army rebirth as an all-round entertainer. Yet Elvis's pre-demob press conference suggested he wasn't going to compromise. 'My attraction for rock 'n' roll hasn't changed one bit and I think it would be a mistake for me to change my style.'

While Elvis fans had shed tears at his parting (*right*), it was clear his popularity had endured despite the arrival of such pseudo-Elvis types as Ricky Nelson from TV's *Ozzie and Harriet*. Colonel Parker underlined his protégé's unique status on his return to US soil with a $150,000 non-negotiable price tag for concert performances after the National Association of Record Merchants named him America's best-selling recording artist.

Elvis's army service abroad had its compensations –
and most notable among these was meeting Priscilla
Beaulieu, the beautiful young daughter of an Air
Force Major. They met and started their courtship in
August 1959, but the fact that she was just fourteen
years old inevitably cooled the romance down for

some while. Elvis's one-time Memphis sweetheart,
Anita Wood, had by this time faded into the back-
ground, though Elvis insisted Priscilla was 'nothing
serious. I can promise you, there's no big
romance!'

They finally married at 9.41 a.m. on 1 May 1967 in
Las Vegas (*right*), though the course of true love
was never to run smooth. 'It wasn't until I reached
30 that I realized that there was a whole other world
out there,' Priscilla said of their years together. 'I
didn't really know how to relate to other people
because I'd been so secluded and sheltered during
my relationship with Elvis.'

Sincerely
Elvis Presley

Hound Dog Goes Hollywood

BY SPENDING THE REQUISITE two years in the service of his country, Elvis had won acceptance from a wider audience and thus laid the groundwork for a career as an all-round entertainer. It was by no means certain, after all, that rock 'n' roll would endure; Colonel Parker's fail-safe policy took account of that possibility, but for a while the music still came first. The album Elvis cut immediately after demobilization, *Elvis Is Back,* is still reckoned to be his best ever. The first single release, 'Stuck On You', shot to Number One as if he'd never been away, assisted by a performance on *The Frank Sinatra Show.* Cut in Nashville in March 1960, it went on sale locally within forty-eight hours of recording.

Fittingly, *GI Blues* opened Presley's post-Army film career in 1960 (ironically putting him back in uniform a mere month after his demob) and set the tone for the celluloid decade to come. Elvis starred as, of all things, a soldier stationed in West Germany, where, in a departure from the real-life script, he fell for a night-club dancer. Songs and many misunderstandings followed, along with the obligatory happy ending.

The movie's big song was 'Wooden Heart', a number far removed from the rabble-rousing rock of pre-army days and one he sang not to co-star Juliet Prowse (*above and right*) but to a puppet! Nevertheless, the track sold two million copies in Germany, where they obviously regarded him as an adopted son, and reached the top of the charts in Britain as well.

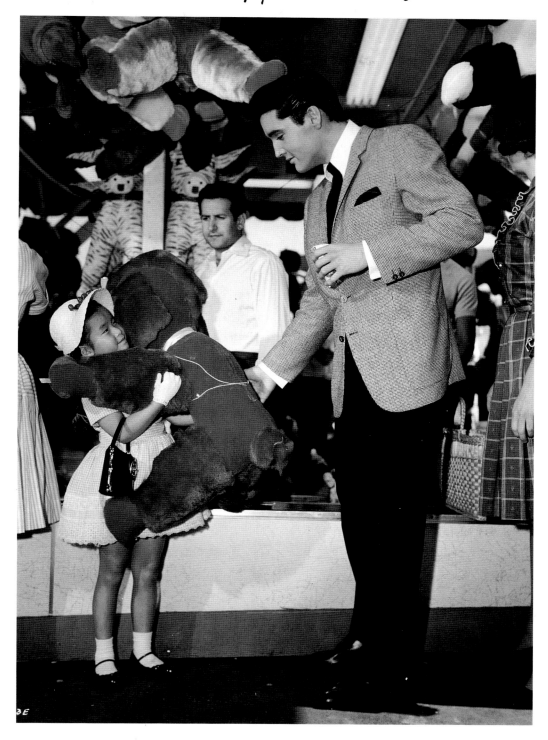

During the twelve civilian years in the period 1956–69 Presley appeared in thirty-one films. The plots were reduced to Elvis in some macho profession (boxer, biker, pilot) put through a series of romantic assignations in photogenic settings (Acapulco, Las Vegas, Hawaii). *Stay Away Joe* in 1968 (*left*) cast him as a half-Indian rodeo rider anxious to secure the future of his parents' reservation. Five years earlier *It Happened At The World's Fair* (*above*) saw him acting with children and (stuffed) animals.

Flaming Star, shot in 1960 (*below and right*), cast Elvis as a half-breed Native American, while the following year's *Wild In The Country* was the second movie to feature just a handful of songs and cast him as something of a James Dean-type country boy with aspirations.

Elvis's screen career was very lucrative. Movie earnings while on set were estimated at some $10,000 per day, adding to his record revenue and royalties of 2.5 per cent on all souvenirs marketed in his name, ranging from jewellery through soft toys to stationery.

Twenty-five of Presley's films were shot from 1961 onwards, when he was unencumbered by the chore of performing live. In retrospect, it's apparent that this machine-like output also had the effect of making his music less exciting, especially since his records were mainly sound-track albums. Only three 'original' albums surfaced, one a gospel effort, the Grammy-winning *How Great Thou Art* in 1967.

Presley's fifteenth film, *Viva Las Vegas* (*left*), saw him co-starring as Lucky Jordan opposite Ann-Margret's Rusty Martin. He was a racing car driver, she a swimming instructor, and the songs included a duet between the two leading characters entitled 'The Lady Loves Me'. Gossip columnists were quick to scent a real-life romance, though Ann-Margret's apparent intimation that wedding plans were in the offing understandably didn't go down too well with Presley's female fans.

The film was curiously retitled *Love In Las Vegas* for the British market, and was well received on both sides of the Atlantic. The fast-moving action centred round Lucky's ambition to drive in the Grand Prix, something he aimed to finance by a run of good fortune at the gambling table. Approached by Count Mancini (played by Cesare Danova) to throw the race, Elvis's search for Rusty, after a chance meeting at a garage when she drops in for running repairs, sets up a clash with Mancini, whom he finds also searching for the girl.

Released in 1964, *Viva Las Vegas* was a good example of how a half-decent script, good direction and a good cast could entertain despite a singular lack of genuine drama.

Blue Hawaii provided 1961's fastest-selling record album in the States, while the film's first run grossed a tidy $4.7 million. The plot was slight, the main attraction Elvis in a swimsuit (*above*), and the escapist mood made the film more popular than subsequent, heavier efforts, like *Kid Galahad*, and produced the blueprint for *Girls! Girls! Girls!,* also filmed in Hawaii and released in 1962. It was a production line of sorts, but a highly successful one, and one that enabled Elvis in February 1963 to renew his RCA

contract for another lucrative ten years.

Though 1968's *Speedway* (*above*) had a slim plot, it co-starred Nancy Sinatra, whose father's TV shows Elvis had graced in his pre-Hollywood period. The pairing represented a coup in that Nancy was then one of the most popular female vocalists. Set in the 'dare-devil world of stock-car racing', it was the eighth Presley movie to be directed by Norman Taurog and featured Bill 'Incredible Hulk' Bixby among its supporting cast.

It Happened At The World's Fair was the first of Presley's two films in 1963, along with *Fun In Acapulco.* Like most of his releases, it combined macho posing (*right*, with Harley Davidson motorcycle) and soft-centred compassion, this time shown for a cute child co-star lost at the Seattle World's Fair.

By the time *Roustabout* was released in 1964, all but the most resolute Elvis fans were becoming concerned that Elvis's movies had become just a *little* predictable. *Kissin Cousins,* shot in just seventeen days, was the turning point, according to Elvis's double, Lance Le Gault. 'Up until then certain standards had been maintained. Once they realized we could do a film so quickly, we were on fast pictures.'

It seemed that Elvis's popularity remained high despite the effects the Hollywood machine had had on his music. In 1966 his popularity in Britain was still such that he could walk away with the Musical Personality award from *New Musical Express* readers in their annual poll despite the presence of more 'modern' artists like the Beatles, Rolling Stones and the Beach Boys.

Not that he could ignore the new generation altogether, as RCA's accountants could doubtless tell him. By this time, his singles and albums usually made the Top Twenty on both sides of the Atlantic, though Top Three hits were rare: exceptions were 1963's 'Devil In Disguise' and 1965's 'Crying In The Chapel'. Film commitments had already reduced his live work to two 1961 charity shows in Memphis and Pearl Harbor, Hawaii, and these were to remain his only Sixties performances for seven years.

Given these restrictions, the films were being asked to do an awful lot of work. And it's a tribute to Presley's reputation and fan following that he retained a presence in pop's major markets despite being unable to promote his releases in person: even the Beatles continued live performances until the mid-Sixties.

Girls! Girls! Girls! (above) saw Elvis take to the high
seas in 1962 in company of a bevy of beauties, a
typical formula film from his early career. By 1968,
however, the scenario had changed. With a live
come-back in the air, 1969's *Change of Habit (right)*,
the last of the feature films, emerged almost unno-
ticed despite the presence of well-known co-star
Mary Tyler Moore. It featured Presley as a socially
responsible slum doctor, suggesting that he was
trying – too late, some said – to give his image some
variety. By this time, falling box-office receipts had
caused film companies to look twice at Colonel
Parker's still substantial financial demands, which
reputedly included a million-dollar guarantee.

Marriage to Priscilla Beaulieu and the birth of only daughter Lisa Marie (*left*) exactly nine months later on 1 February 1967 at Memphis's Baptist Memorial Hospital clearly rejuvenated Elvis. He prepared to re-enter the fray, and Colonel Parker's chosen vehicle was a TV special on the giant NBC network. The build-up included another eagerly awaited event: Elvis's first press conference. 'We figured it was about time,' he joked to journalists about his return to the stage, adding 'Besides, I thought I'd better do it before I got too old.'

The show was taped between 27 and 29 June 1968 and broadcast on 3 December of that year. A slim-line, black-leather-clad Elvis had promised that this would be no variety show: he'd 'sing, almost exclusively…and sing the songs I'm known for'. Though, as Colonel Parker pointed out, 'if he did that, that would take *hours*…NBC only gave us an hour.' Material ranged from the current hit 'If I Can Dream' (whose sales hit the million mark) to golden oldies like 'Don't Be Cruel', 'Jailhouse Rock', Heartbreak Hotel' and 'Are You Lonesome Tonight?'. All were tackled with the gusto of a man released from solitary confinement. *New Musical Express*'s New York correspondent reported that 'Elvis at 33 is sensational…he still sings those Memphis blues like they've just been written', concluding 'After a twelve-year gap, Elvis's second career starts from the top.'

Director Steve Binder had instructed Presley to return to his roots and create a show that reflected the energy of the Sun years and the rock 'n' roll image of yore. The sky-high viewing figures confirmed the strategy to be a no-holds-barred success – and, just as importantly, renewed Elvis's appetite for performing live. It is no exaggeration to state that this one performance set the style for Elvis's subsequent career. Hollywood was now in the past: serious recording and live performance was henceforth the order of the day.

Graceland, Graceland

THE PRESLEYS made their home at Graceland, where they lived a cloistered existence, protected from the media spotlight by an entourage known as the 'Memphis Mafia' (*overleaf*).

Priscilla later recalled their sheltered life there. 'I accepted his way of life as normal. When I was older I realized that not everybody sat in dark rooms and had their food brought up to them, but that was just our way of life. His sleeping habits were the opposite of everyone else's, so I had to adjust to those habits. ...it was very difficult for him to get out and do things.'

Graceland was sumptuously appointed, and contained a recording studio, where Elvis cut his final releases, *From Elvis Presley Boulevard* (1976) and *Moody Blue* (1977).

With his NBC special having proved that Elvis's on-stage magic remained, the obvious next move was to jump off the sound-track treadmill and resume a rock 'n' roll recording career. In January 1969 Elvis entered Memphis's American Studios, where newer names, like Dusty Springfield and Neil Diamond (to name but two), had produced some of their best work.

In just sixteen days Elvis got his musical career back on the tracks and hustling forwards. Although nursing a sore throat, he turned in some epic vocal performances, and from these came no fewer than four million-selling singles – 'In The Ghetto', 'Suspicious Minds', 'Don't Cry Daddy', 'Rubberneckin'' and 'Kentucky Rain' – and two gold

albums: *From Elvis In Memphis* and the studio part of *From Memphis To Vegas.* It was clear the Midas touch remained, and it wasn't just Tom Parker that was pleased about that!

It was the first time Elvis had recorded in Memphis since the Sun days, and it was as if all the fans he'd gathered since then had come out of the woodwork. From then onwards, hit singles like 'The Wonder Of You', 'Burning Love', 'Always On My Mind' and 'My Boy' alternated with musical projects, like *Elvis Country,* that reflected not only a new appetite for recording but an interest in the material he was choosing. Elvis was reborn, in a recording sense, and that was good news for everyone. Hollywood's loss was the music business's gain.

The success of the TV showcase emboldened the King to take another look at his subjects, and plans were laid for a live come-back. The venue was to be Las Vegas, home of the glamorous and glitzy, and the venue for his own wedding just two years before. Elvis had wanted to tour, but Colonel Parker had other ideas, setting up a contract to play Vegas's International Hotel for twenty-eight days, two shows a night, in July 1969. In terms of endurance, it was every bit as tough as a tour. The opening night (*above*) was Elvis's first live performance to a paying audience in nine years.

He confounded the critics with material ranging

from 'Blue Suede Shoes' to the still-new 'In The Ghetto'. The 2,000-seat main showroom applauded as one, giving him no fewer than four standing ovations at the end of his hour-long first performance. 'I don't think I've ever been more excited than I was last night,' he told the following day's press conference, adding 'I'm really glad to be back in front of a live audience.' And successive audiences showed they were happy to have him back too.

Fellow star Francoise Hardy paid fulsome tribute: 'All those tight suits look sexy on him. It's unbelievable to think he's 34. I can't think of anybody but Elvis I'd put myself in trouble for.'

Colonel Parker had been correct in assuming a TV special would prove the most effective way in re-awakening 'Elvis fever' across the nation – indeed, across the world. And even though the King had returned to live performance, Parker wasn't going to let a good idea get away. Two 'on the road' documentaries, 1970's *Elvis: That's The Way It Is* and the 1972 *Elvis On Tour,* proved perfect showcases for the man and his rejuvenated music. The latter, incorporating historic footage of an early *Ed Sullivan Show* appearance as well as of some inspired improvisation in rehearsal with a gospel quartet, which caught Elvis at his most natural, even won the coveted Golden Globe Award for Best Documentary of the Year in 1972.

Presley's 1972 band was a particularly hot one. In place of Sun six-stringer Scotty Moore, he had an equally able first lieutenant in James Burton, who'd ironically climbed to fame on the shoulders of prime Presley substitute Ricky Nelson when Elvis had been in the army. Glen D. Hardin on piano was another important segment of the instrumental backbone that held the King's crown in place, with a rhythm section of Jerry Scheff (bass) and Ron Tutt (drums). Vocal backing was provided by the Sweet Inspirations, who'd also been around in 1970, while guitarists Charlie Hodges and John Wilkinson made up the numbers.

Elvis's personal behaviour off-stage had been giving cause for concern. Bizarrely, in 1970 he'd asked Richard Nixon to make him a federal narcotics officer, having turned up at the White House and handed a handwritten note to a security guard. Being Elvis, he was granted his wish (*right*).

At this point, even if he displayed a certain amount of eccentricity, he was at least in perfect physical shape for a man in his mid-thirties. For many fans, it would be the lack of physical self-discipline that would sadly characterize the mid-Seventies Elvis. While Priscilla was around, however, he clearly had reason to take pride in his appearance.

When the Big Apple played host to the King, bill-
boards were hung out around Times Square to
welcome him for what were, incredibly, his first
ever New York dates: a three-night residency at
Madison Square Garden on 9–11 June 1972.
Typically, Tom Parker vetoed the idea of compli-
mentary tickets, so even the most stellar of the star-
studded 80,000 audience had to pay to get in. This
led to some entertaining situations: people sitting at
the back of the stalls found themselves rubbing
shoulders with John Lennon and Bob Dylan, while a
second ex-Beatle, George Harrison, had to be
content with a mere balcony view. The mayor of

New York was there, too – though no one quite knew where – to see Elvis on the very top of his form.

Perhaps Presley's most famous Seventies' performance renewed his connections with Hawaii, such a popular backdrop for his Sixties movies. His *Aloha From Hawaii* show of 14 January 1973 was simultaneously broadcast to a huge worldwide audience of 500 million in some forty countries. Seventeen years later came a second album of out-takes, *The Alternative Aloha* – and even then the King's magnetism was still strong enough to inspire healthy sales of what owned up to being a second-string album.

Elvis doted on his young wife (*below*) and daughter, so it was inevitable that when Priscilla finally rebelled against the lifestyle imposed upon her the decision would hit him hard. The divorce decree was granted on 9 October 1973 in Santa Monica, California, on the grounds of irreconcilable differences – one significant one being karate teacher Mike Stone, with whom Priscilla was reported to be

living. Ironically, the martial arts were a Presley passion. Elvis's lawyer reported, 'The reason for the divorce is that Elvis has been spending six months a year on the road, which put a tremendous strain on the marriage.'

Priscilla, who retained the Presley surname as well as her own maiden name of Beaulieu, subsequently managed to create a reputation in her own right as a TV and movie actress of note. In the Eighties she played the glamorous Jenna Wade in the TV soap opera *Dallas*. Perhaps the role came naturally after having played a part in what must have seemed like the most bizarre soap opera of all time. And far from estranging herself from the memory of her former husband, she played as active a part as she could in ensuring that the many posthumous film tributes were respectful rather than exploitative.

The newly single Presley dated a number of women after the split, including actresses Tuesday Weld and Natalie Wood, before Linda Thompson became his long-term girlfriend. When not touring, he was a virtual recluse at Graceland, with the infamous Memphis Mafia never far away. Elvis stories, many apocryphal and all sad, abounded: he memorized all James Dean's dialogue in the Fifties' classic *Rebel Without A Cause* and summoned the film's director so he could recite it, word perfect. He fired a gun at a television during a performance by singer Robert Goulet that annoyed him. What was certain was that he never, ever granted interviews, so no rebuttal ever came, though his jowly and bloated appearance spoke volumes even tailored stage wear couldn't hope to hide.

It seems that towards the end of his life Elvis became intrigued by the solutions offered by different religions, even investigating Eastern beliefs in the person of Yogi Paramahansa Yogananda. Just prior to his death, it was said, he'd been studying a book entitled *The Scientific Search for the Face of Jesus*. Whatever the truth, it seemed certain he was more in need of guidance than at any time in his life. Surrounded by opulence and 'yes men', he lacked the sound advice required to steer a course through the junk food, television and prescription drugs that apparently dominated his life.

After Elvis and Priscilla (*above*, at a party with Frank Sinatra and Fred Astaire) split, Elvis remained in seclusion when he wasn't working. In the early days of hip-swivelling and public indignation, the producers of Steve Allen's TV show had had Elvis singing 'Hound Dog', dressed in tails, to a basset hound on a pedestal. Even that had failed to tame America's hottest rocker. Now, it seemed, he had all but tamed himself, emerging from his lair only to stalk the stage in search of yesterday's memories.

As the Seventies progressed, Elvis's shows started to be cancelled due to illness, and such was the lack of newly recorded product that RCA in Britain solved the problem by using old LP tracks as new singles. 'Suspicion' and 'The Girl Of My Best Friend' both re-established Presley's chart credentials in this way, reaching the UK Top Ten in 1976, and were followed by the newly recorded 'Moody Blue', a Number Six hit in 1977.

By late 1974 rumours were rife in the less salubrious newspapers that Elvis was sick, dying, drug-ridden or gay. Illegitimate children and terminal cancer were two of the most often quoted and totally untrue rumours peddled by at least two dozen magazines. Unfortunately, the accusations struck a nerve. In a season at the Las Vegas Hilton Elvis denounced his critics from the stage, accusing hotel waiters and porters of feeding information to the press. During the between-song ramblings, which became longer and longer, he showed the audience his narcotics bureau badge as proof he'd never taken drugs. And Priscilla herself went public on their 'conventional' love life in a series of syndicated newspaper articles intended to quell exotic rumours.

The post-divorce years saw him throwing himself into his work and fulfilling a schedule many younger stars would have had trouble keeping up with. Between 17 March 1975 and 1 January 1976 Elvis toured seventy-four cities, often playing multiple dates, jetting round the country in his Convair 880 airliner named after his daughter. His stage swansong was a CBS TV special in the summer of 1977, ironically hailed as his finest performance in years.

His health was deteriorating fast. In the last four years of his life he was hospitalized five times for everything from flu and fatigue to eye and intestinal problems. After his death, a hospital employee told reporters 'Elvis had the arteries of an 80-year-old man. His body was just worn out.'

Like many other rock fatalities, Elvis Presley's demise was far from unpredictable. Yet rather than debasing his memory, the declining Graceland years have come to be regarded as a regrettable postscript to a remarkable career.

Elvis continues to inspire tributes in print and in song from artists as major as Paul Simon (*Graceland*) and Marc Cohn ('Walking In Memphis'). Another burgeoning Elvis-related activity is impersonation: when the King inspired so many singers in his heyday, it was hardly surprising that another generation attempted to fill the gap.

Despite innumerable attempts to taint it or cash in on it with films, records and unsavoury book and magazine revelations, the Elvis Presley legend has proved to be stronger than mere flesh and blood.

Rock deaths have sold millions of records, and the untimely departures of such as Buddy Holly and John Lennon have led to speculation as to what they would have accomplished had they survived to create more music. In Elvis Presley's case immortality was already more than assured. To many, he *was* rock 'n' roll. And though stories persist in the lower orders of the press that he is alive and well and living as a recluse, it seems certain that he died in the early hours of 16 August 1977 in a Graceland bathroom.

Graceland (*left and above left*) located on the south side of Memphis on Highway 51, had once been a happy family home, then a refuge from the media and, finally, a hideaway for Elvis in his reclusive days. Now it became a shrine to his memory and a mecca for Elvis fans the world over, visited by thousands yearly. Over 75,000 people attended his funeral, where National Guardsmen formed an honour guard and even the Soviet Union sent a wreath. Millions more put him back at the top of the charts worldwide: 'Way Down' was his first UK Number One for seven years.

The fact that Elvis Presley's record sales exceeded 300 million by the end of the Seventies would alone guarantee him a place in rock history books. But mere sales figures or Grammy awards – four of them, including one in 1971 for 'creative contributions of outstanding significance' – are not nearly enough to measure the impact and influence of the man.

Back in the late Fifties Buddy Holly was acknowledging him as the founding father of rock: 'Without Elvis, none of us could have made it.' On his death, President Jimmy Carter claimed that 'Elvis Presley's death deprives our country of a part of itself.'

But Elvis's special relevance to America was more than that. Just as surely as the man in the White House, he represented the essential American Dream – that someone from lowly estate could, given the necessary gifts, guts and determination, become an all-powerful figure. Though his demise showed how the American Dream could turn sour, somehow the Elvis Presley legend would never lose its lustre.

Acknowledgements

Managing Editor: Lesley McOwan
Design: Robert Mathias
Production: Nick Thompson
Picture Research: Emily Hedges
Editor: Barbara Horn

The Publishers should like to thank the following organizations for their kind permission to reproduce the photographs in this book:-

Aquarius Picture Library; 52, 55, 56, 58, 62 left, 62-63, 70, 84, 85; Camera Press; 76-77, /Gilloon; 10-11, 29, /Ray Hamilton; 90-91; The Ronald Grant Archive; 34-35, 41; The Hulton Picture Company; 50, / Bettmann Archive; 36-37, 38-39; Katz Photos /Snap Photo/JR; 5, 23, 26, 27, 40; The Kobal Collection; 6, 12-13, 24-25, 28, 57, 59, 60, 65, 66, 67; London Features International; 18, 19, 20, 21, 44 top and bottom, 72-73, 77 right, 95, 96, /Michael Ochs Archive; 16, 22; Popperfoto; 42, 43, 46-47, 68, 76 left, 80-81, 81 right, 82-83; Rex Features; 3, 9, 48, 61, 74, 75, 79, 86-87, 88-89, /Globe; 91 right, /Images/J Schwartz; 30-31, /Photoplay Archives; 14,/Sipa; 15, 34 left, 37 right, /Sipa/Ried; 92-93, 94; Topham Picture Source; 32, 45, 49, 51, 54.